Display
for
Learning

371.335/AND

Also available from Network Continuum

Towards Successful Learning (second edition) – Diane Pardoe

Display
for
Learning

Kirstie Andrew-Power and Charlotte Gormley

network
continuum

Continuum International Publishing Group

Network Continuum
The Tower Building   80 Maiden Lane, Suite 704
11 York Road   New York
SE1 7NX   NY 10038

www.networkcontinuum.co.uk
www.continuumbooks.com

British Library Cataloguing-in-Publication Data
A catalogue record for this book is available from the British Library.

ISBN: 9781855394506 (paperback)

Library of Congress Cataloguing-in-Publication Data
A catalog record for this book is available from the Library of Congress.

Photographs provided by Mark Green
www.greenimages.com

Typeset by Ben Cracknell Studios | www.benstudios.co.uk
Printed and bound in Great Britain by Ashford Colour Press Ltd, Gosport, Hampshire

Contents

Acknowledgements

The authors dedicate their work to Teresa Tunnadine: an inspirational leader, role model and friend.

The authors would like to acknowledge and thank colleagues and friends who have influenced their work on display and environments for learning, and those who have directly contributed to this book:

Teresa Tunnadine, Louise Taylor, Hannah Lewis, Clare Foster, Judy Power, Jane Brighton, Nick Brighton, Shalley Lewis, James Gormley, Elaine Turner, Rosanna Raimato, Mike Fleetham, Bridget Gribbs, Robin Gormley, Sarah Beanland, Debbie Morgan, Carolyn Terry, Mick O'Leary, Denise Beardshaw, Ann Marie Mulkerins, Malcolm McGlynn, David Crossley, Professor Alma Harris, Alastair Smith and Sir Alan Steer.

Staff and students at The Compton School; Ani Magill, Headteacher and staff and students at St John the Baptist School, Woking; Christine Owen, Headteacher and staff and students at Bartley Green School, Birmingham; Steve Hillbourne, Headteacher and staff and students at The Manorside Primary School, Barnet; Rhodri Bryan, Headteacher and staff and students at Longdean School, Hertfordshire; Iain Hulland, Headteacher and staff and students at Alder Grange School, Rossendale; Mrs Edwards, Northwick Manor Primary School; Ms Thorpe, Bishop Perowne High School and Mark Green for supplying such fantastic photographs.

All our love and thanks to Tom, Sam and Phoebe and to Noah.

Introduction

According to popular psychology, we form an opinion about a person within two minutes of meeting them. It follows, then, that we judge the character of a school in this time, and what leads to forming these opinions is the focus of this book. We asked a group of Ofsted inspectors about this; they said that the reception area in a school enabled them to form an opinion regarding a school's ethos. Graffiti, peeling paint, torn posters, out-of-date notices and closed doors were the negatives; the positives they cited were pictures, tidiness, plants, photographs, certificates and smiles. Walking through an entrance hall to a school speaks volumes about its ethos; as visitors, parents, students, staff or prospective staff we form an opinion about the school based on what we first see. In schools where this first impression exudes the positive, display celebrates achievement and success, there are images of happy learners, learning-focused signs and statements and the environment seems cared for and respected. In others negative statements confront visitors, the environment is neglected and unloved, and there are no references to learning in the entrance to the school.

Our vision is to share our learning through five years of work on display and environments across schools, to provide you with support materials to develop, further develop and transform display and environment in your classroom and school. This has grown from what we wished we could find: a guide, packed full of ideas for classroom display, corridor display, how to move beyond simply displaying students' work to creating display that enhances and enables learning, how to nurture staff confidence and belief in the importance of environments conducive to learning, and how to enable school leaders to achieve consistency without making onerous demands on staff time and energy.

This is a teachers' toolkit to enable you to create classroom environments that embrace learning, to set a future vision, and it is a book that can be picked up and used whenever you need ideas. Whether this is on a shoestring or with significant resources behind it, for every idea you see here, you will find ten of your own. It is a practical guide for developing display and environments *across* the school, and a powerful tool for school leaders who are committed to distributed leadership and enhanced student engagement. Your best advocates will be those passionate about the impact environments and display can have on learning and every child; if you are one of these people, we wrote this with you in mind. You will inspire future generations of teachers and students to achieve their very best in an environment where they feel nurtured and cared for, where they belong and where their successes are celebrated and recognized.

Environment and display send these powerful messages and this book aims to capture how and why we should provide these to enable every child to succeed. Anything is possible at classroom or whole-school level – and every development makes a difference to this learning ethos.

Display for learning – what you get . . .

- practical tips for classroom display – generic and subject specific
- advice on how to utilize display to enhance learning
- examples of how display and environments support the embedding of whole-school developments
- approaches that work *with* workforce agreements
- ideas and strategies in working with staff to distribute leadership and move towards consistency
- student voice and engagement activities
- practical tips for corridor display
- practical ideas for reflecting your school ethos through display
- practical ideas for promoting achievement and celebration through display
- practical ways to utilize display to show that every child truly matters in your school

The current educational climate places learner well-being as core to enabling every child to achieve their very best, and we assert throughout that display and environment play a key role here. It is reassuring to see this in black and white in The Children's Plan,[1] where various references highlight how the environment in every classroom supports effective teaching and learning, referring to the physical environment *and* the environment that is created by the school and the teacher.

We explore wide-ranging, practical approaches, moving on from simply displaying students' work to creating effective display *for learning* and utilizing the whole school environment to enable and enhance learning. We draw from our experience as classroom teachers, senior leaders and working across primary and secondary schools. Our experience of developing a whole-school approach to display and environment for learning at The Compton School in Barnet[2] has formed the basis of all our development work with this agenda.

We share our learning and draw from ideas and strategies on which students and staff have worked together, motivated by a desire to create learning environments where we all want to be, that support the school's core beliefs and values and provide the best possible opportunities for all in the school community. We also draw on how this learning has been replicated, transferred, built on and developed across other schools. This is a practical guide written *for* teachers, school leaders and students, *by* teachers, school leaders and students.

The Classroom

Chapter 1

Getting started

There is no one who knows the curriculum and the students you teach like you do. You have the skills and knowledge to create a display that genuinely makes a difference. Every child matters and this can so easily be articulated through the display you create; in this respect we are passionate in asserting that *every* display matters too. This section is a practical toolkit that will enable you to create displays for your classroom that reflect your passion and desire to teach. For those of you thinking, 'I can't', just add the word 'yet' and read on.

It's all in the planning . . .

Some colleagues we have worked with, although appreciative of the value of display, have found it difficult to create a display that has visual impact and generates interest. If this sounds familiar, then this chapter will support you in developing step-by-step practical advice which includes visual examples to motivate and provoke creativity. You may on the other hand be someone who creates display with visual impact but wants to take it to the next level and use it as a tool to enhance learning – this section will also provide ideas to enable you to utilize display as a teaching tool. The place to start is to plan how you will use display within the classroom as a whole – this list is a useful starting place:

- list each year group and subject that you teach in your classroom
- list the topic areas and themes that you teach
- ask yourself what you want a display for each topic / year group to achieve
- use Google or the National Educational Network Gallery to identify the key visuals that will support the understanding of this topic
- print large pictures or better still try to find 3D objects (see ideas below) that represent these visuals
- use the pictures / 3D shapes to form the basis of your display
- plan the key words, statements and ideas around your key visual

For example, in order to help Key Stage 4 English classes successfully complete analysis of a media text, they need to remember the acronym CLAP: content, language, audience, purpose. The teacher used a large pair of foam hands as the focal point of the display board as the aim was to encourage the students to remember the acronym. The display was built around this initial idea (see Photograph 1 in the plate section).

This example illustrates the impact of visuals on enabling student understanding of fractions. A range of colourful objects that students can relate to are divided up to visually demonstrate the concept. In this example of a display board, the Mathematics teacher has selected a picnic theme, and images and objects linked with this theme were cut up to illustrate the various fractions.

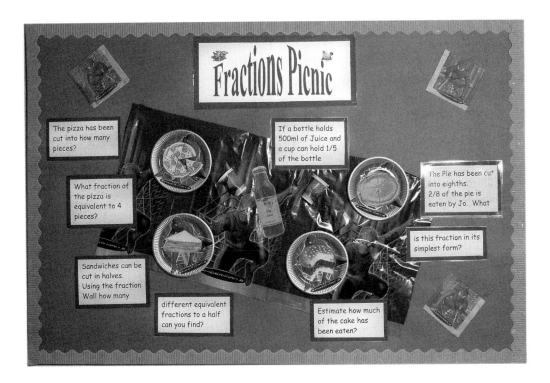

This simple idea shows how the colleague has taken a topic for a year group, planned what the display is aiming to achieve and kept it simple, using large visuals, key words and statements.

An English teacher asked herself what she wanted to achieve through a display board she was preparing; it was to enhance students' understanding of a complex poem based on self-reflection. To encourage students to understand what the metaphorical language was attempting to communicate she uses a lightweight mirror that students are encouraged to look into while the poem is read.

When planning displays eBay becomes your best friend. No matter how bizarre the object it will be listed, from false teeth through to the entire solar system. Once you have your images and ideas you can then plan the display around these roughly on paper. Inspiring display does not just occur by chance. If you plan carefully you will produce display that excites and engages children with the concept you are attempting to teach them. To achieve outstanding lessons, planning is crucial, and when display becomes an intrinsic part of lesson preparation the impact on learning can be significant.

Strip, strip, strip!

Once you have planned what you intend to display you should begin by completely stripping the board of the previous display. It is tempting to cover over previous displays, but this 'time-saving' strategy will end up costing you as the staples and previous bits of card inevitably poke through. Start afresh. Removing staples with scissor blades is not only horribly time-consuming but you could end up removing more than you bargained for, so ensure you are fully equipped. This includes being the sole owner of a flat staple remover, a wall staple gun and staples to fit. Having the correct staples to fit the staple gun should be built into the teacher-training package; it alleviates the majority of stress associated with display and this equipment will allow you to fix your backing card securely to the board, which will not only speed up the process but will provide a facelift for older backing boards.

It's all in the coordination

After the initial planning stages you should next decide on a colour scheme that will complement the theme and build this into your plan. It is all about exciting the visual palette. To start you will need to consider coordinating:

- backing paper/card
- mounting card (see section below)
- border colour/s

As a rule of thumb select opposite colours from the colour wheel; you can find lots of examples of colour wheels on Google Images (type in 'colour wheels' and a range of different ones will come up). Opposites usually work well, but use your professional judgement here and ask yourself if the chosen colours complement the theme of the board and work well together.

Back the board using your chosen cheerful colour. Then for mounting, select the opposite colour on the colour wheel. We generally recommend avoiding yellow, white and beige as backing. Colours that are vivid and eye-catching and work well together are blue and purple, red and green, blue and orange, red and blue and bright colours paired with black. Varying shades of one colour can also work well. There is no need to try to coordinate the boards in your room or make them match; we were both keen on this in our early days but have since moved on, realizing how much more can be achieved without these restraints. Again, revisiting the colour wheel may help you make choices throughout your classroom.

Once you have selected your colours, you can collect your backing materials. A good tip here is to use sheets of card and avoid rolls of paper. It seems to be cheaper but is a false economy. Rolls of paper are difficult to use, look amateur and are not as robust as they need to be. Displays backed using rolls of paper need repairing and replacing often, and time is of the essence. The amount of card you can use will depend on your display budget (we explore this in more detail later in the book) and you may be in a position to have admin support for getting this done for you (again later in the book . . .). Either way, if you take ownership over all display *planning*, including your colour schemes, you will find that you create a classroom environment that supports effective learning and teaching and this is the desired outcome.

Putting up backing card is relatively simple and although there may be the odd lump and bump, don't let this put you off. As long as the card is fixed in straight lines the finished product will be stunning.

Background detail counts

Do not limit yourself by only using card as a backdrop. Wallpaper, fabric, wrapping paper and newspaper are just a few materials that could be used as backgrounds to enhance the display. Always remember that less is more; it is difficult to make very busy dominant backgrounds work.

The example shown in Photograph 2 in the plate section demonstrates how using subtle printed silk as the backdrop captures the vitality of spring.

Another example, taken from the Art Department and shown in Photograph 3 in the plate section, illustrates the effective use of brick wallpaper to successfully capture the street theme. This display highlights that the 'less is more' approach can be very powerful.

In the example from the History Department shown in Photograph 8 in the plate section, a Union Jack flag has been used as the main backdrop and colour-coordinated information cards have been attached over the top.

Each of these backdrops not only adds to the appearance but also encourages the learning process. Students will subconsciously absorb these images, reinforcing the learning taking place in the lesson.

Now your background is done, we explore a range of different ways of producing classroom display. We have included photographs to illustrate ideas and strategies, and explore different techniques that you can use. These form your toolkit, and it is this toolkit that will transform your ability to produce dynamic and effective display.

Mounting – unnecessary or essential?

We fall into the camp of believing that mounting is crucial for quality display. In fact we would assert here that we *know* it is crucial. Although double backing does take time the final result absolutely makes it worthwhile. You will find that once you have opted to go for double-mounted display you will never look back. Careful mounting pulls the text or image you want the students to focus on away from the board. In the example shown in Photograph 4 in the plate section, the poetry is double-backed with orange and black, and this colour combination highlights the text cards. The text box is filled with an orange fading effect and then a white border is left around the outside of the text. This is then backed on black and then orange. The title cards use blue to contrast and this third layer is used to draw the students' eyes to the titles to help them categorize the information. When mounting items to go on the board, begin by mounting with the colour used on the back of the board and then select a complementary colour and back it again.

Breaking the boundaries with borders . . .

Once the content is planned and you have decided on your colour scheme your next challenge is to create the border. While the standard cardboard strips are relatively easy to use, there are many alternative designs that could further enhance your display. Again consider the purpose of the board: what message are you trying to communicate? Select images, words or photographs that enhance this message and place them around the outside of the display, creating a fantastic border.

Using photographs . . .

In the example below, the teacher has selected photographs of herself at poignant moments in her life. These photographs have been reduced on the colour photocopier and repeated strips of the pictures are made into the border. The aim of the display is to enable students to understand the key message from the poem. This is for the reader to consider themselves at various points in their life. As a homework exercise students were asked to reflect on the key message and bring in photographs of themselves, and suddenly an imaginary exercise came to life. The photograph below shows how strips can be used both vertically and horizontally, another tip for varying your borders.

One teacher asked students how exams made them feel and photographed each one of them pulling the various faces with a digital camera. These photographs were then downloaded, re-sized and cut into strips, then made into a border for a display encouraging effective revision for Key Stage 4 students. This was not just a revision board but an entertaining and engaging display created by students, for students.

Simple images are not only effective for visual learners who will associate the symbol with the topic, but using images of students also communicates that everyone is a valued member of the classroom community. Display boards that reinforce positive behaviour rules become more powerful when photographs of students following them are included. In the example below you can see that the borders are made up of images of students following the 'golden rules' regarding the uniform policy. This positive reinforcement encourages positive relationships and a culture of positive behaviour.

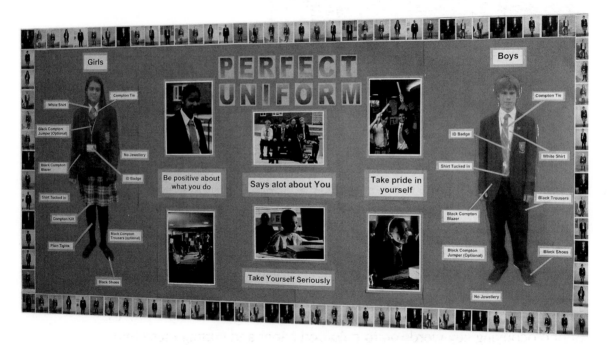

Using words . . .

While personalized photograph borders are an incredibly powerful way to communicate a message, words or images can also have the desired effect. In the example on the next page, Gujarati is used to emphasize the celebration of cultural identity.

Borders can be created using repeated key words, again a simple process
of photocopying key words on to coloured paper and cutting these into
strips. One Maths classroom has the key words for each year group as the
border for their display board. Students in a Year 9 group were asked to
record words that made them feel proud and motivated. These words were
typed, copied on coloured paper and form the border for the tutor group
display board, providing a daily dose of positive encouragement and a
sense of belonging. This example triggered a colleague in PE to ask her
students to record all the positive words they knew about exercise. These
were again typed, copied on to coloured paper and formed the border

for the board in the sports hall. Again a simple concept, but a reinforced message to all learners abut the positive benefits of exercise.

This technique can be used to advertise key words, statements, messages, spellings; these become silent prompts for all learners and are a simple, cheap and efficient way of producing appealing borders.

Creative borders . . .

Borders do not only have to be fixed to the edges of the board. In this example strips of paper used at the edge of the board have been stapled to create waves that have real visual impact. This type of border is simple and effective to produce. This is creativity at its best; who said everything had to be stapled flat?

The border in the example shown in Photograph 5 in the plate section. comes away from the board. Using raindrops on transparent strips of plastic reinforces that the display is about the water cycle.

Simple repeated images such as the witches across the bottom of the Trial and Terror board immediately capture what this display is about. More intricate borders can be seen in the agriculture/industry board, shown in Photograph 12 in the plate section. The teacher has included a variety of small shapes, stripes and images to capture the era. These were collected from Google Images and blown up on the photocopier. Other images used in display can be cut from newspapers and magazines, or, as in this example, a large arrow cut out from card.

Font size 72 as a minimum . . .

Now that you have all of the basic images in mind you will next need to consider how you intend to display information. Although it is stating the obvious, it is worth highlighting this as an important point: masses of small writing has almost no effect at all. In our enthusiasm to ensure we have as much information as possible on classroom display boards (as some of us do with PowerPoint presentations . . .) we lose sight of the need to be concise, clear and direct. Ensure text can be read otherwise it is of no value. The rule of thumb is that titles and keywords should be no less than font size 72. Sticking to this forces you to be concise. In this example, keywords are used to inform the images. This is a useful technique and supports different learning styles with the combination of text and pictures.

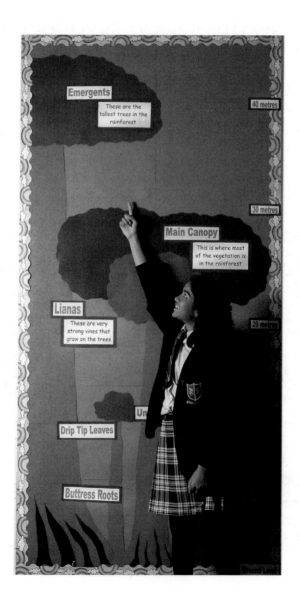

Using black but wisely . . .

Both of us were initially drawn to the dark side (walls of black card) in our first introductions to the world of display. Black is a tricky colour to use and if used badly can drain the room of energy. The following examples (although in black and white) show how effective using black can be, if used alongside contrasting colours. The *La Haine* board, shown in Photograph 6 in the plate section, uses four key colours that complement one another. The simple black silhouettes stand out from the grey background and the contrasting use of white highlights the commentary cards. The windows in the tower blocks are blocked in yellow, as is the fire, which is also tinted with orange. The introduction of yellow and orange is subtle but instantly lights up the buildings.

Both the Horror Story and the Propaganda display boards below and overleaf illustrate the effective use of shapes on a contrasting background; simple silhouette images create highly effective displays. You do not have to be a skilled artist to achieve work of this standard. These images were found using Google then projected on to the interactive whiteboard and traced on to paper from the screen (this is a job that many willing Year 8s and 9s are keen to help with). Once on paper the image can then be cut out and used as a stencil. The stencil can then be used on any material, which is then cut and transferred on to the display board.

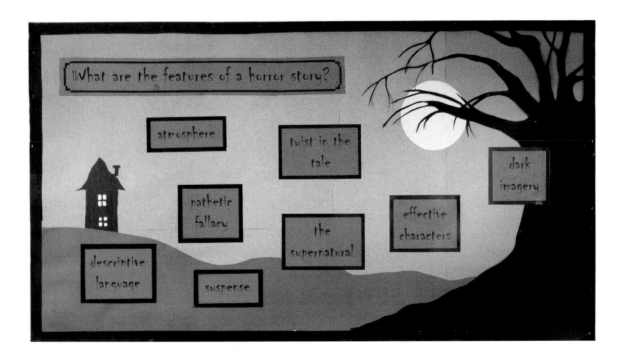

Displaying titles

Banners (font size 72 or more) seem to be the most popular method for displaying a title, but there are lots of other creative methods. In the examples below and on the next page, individual letters have been attached to a strip of paper that hangs away from the board. Each individual letter is printed on to images that relate to the title. For example, each letter of the word 'lamb' is printed in bold over the top of lambs in a field (below) and each letter of the word 'shower' is printed over the image of an umbrella (on the next page).

You can also fill the letters themselves with relevant symbols, as can be seen in the Mathematics example below that includes repeated images of calculators, percentage signs, scales, etc.

Using shapes for titles . . . thinking outside the box

Try to use alternative shapes other than boxes for displaying titles and/or written information. In the What is History? display below the teacher has used magnifying glass shapes to frame the title, and this is then repeated for key words. This is a simple technique that makes the display visually engaging, more so than using the standard text box shape. The student is able to draw links between the investigative skills required for this particular part of the course through the imagery used.

We have also seen this technique used in Science, where titles are presented in large cut-outs of Bunsen burners, test tubes and thermometer shapes.

Checklist 1

- you have now planned which topic/year group you want your board to focus on and clarified what you want the display to achieve
- you have planned your colour schemes and started experimenting with contrast
- you have planned and prepared your key visual/s, key words and statements and made these exciting, double-mounting them using your complementary colours
- you have planned and prepared a visually stimulating border
- you have backed your display board . . .

Chapter 2

Getting creative

Now it is time to start building your display and this gives a fantastic opportunity to be creative. The key message here is to push the boundaries, and you do not need to be artistic to do this. All good teachers are creative, and it is tapping into this creative streak that will enable you to make display with impact. We remembered another mistake we made in the early part of our teaching careers: only using square images neatly presented in rows on the board, and restricting our work to the confines of the border, so the first message is to be daring. Overlap images; do not be restricted by the frame of the board; spill images out on to the windows or walls. Message two is to be confident in breaking away from using *only* the traditional; bullet points, squares and boxes and straight lines are all important but not essential. In the example below you can see that clipboards have been used to summarize the feedback from Ofsted rather than a traditional typed bullet-point or text-box approach. This example also shows how the teacher has used a repeat image of the Ofsted 'outstanding' logo as the border, photocopied as a black-and-white repeat image. Not only is this a visually exciting stimulus but it also communicates the grading received, which is the fundamental purpose of the board.

Creativity at the display board . . .

Message three is to explore using 3D materials on the display boards. This has liberated how colleagues have used display across the schools we have worked with. Students are drawn towards boards that they can touch and many of our colleagues now completely avoid flat display. Objects can be used for a variety of purposes to enhance learning, including the introduction of discussion work. At the beginning of the GCSE Art course students debate 'What is Art?' The board in the example below includes a selection of objects that have featured in art galleries, ranging from a gargoyle through to a traditional framed oil painting. Students are asked to identify objects that they believe have a place in a gallery and present arguments for the case. This board is easily recreated by engaging students; inviting them to bring in an object that they consider to be art, giving them ownership over the development of the display and generating further debate and discussion.

We have found that novels lend themselves well to display. Teaching staff in the English department considered the visuals required to highlight the central themes in *Lord of the Flies* (opposite). Foliage, flies and a pig mask were used to illustrate the brutality of the killing of the sow. Wearing the pig mask while thirty students chant 'Kill the pig, cut its throat, spill its blood' is an unnerving but highly engaging task that demonstrates the total collapse of law and order in the book. Having the pig mask at the centre of the display allowed the teacher to use it in a number of lessons, and this enabled the exploration of the breakdown of civilization through the engaging chanting task.

The use of the spider in this ICT networks web (below) is dramatic and has really encouraged students to engage with it. If we go back to the final three points in our original list 'It's all in the planning . . .' we can see how this display board has evolved. The ICT team wanted the display board to reinforce key words and build students' confidence with this language. They chose a dramatic key visual, the spider, then built around this visual with key words and statements, using the spider's web as a washing line. The titles, flags and key words are fixed at different angles, some are wavy, images spill outside the borders and the overall effect is dramatic and exciting. The board has been built with a specific scheme of work in mind and is used as a starter activity to link, the intention being that the definition card is matched with the key word, reinforcing meaning and concept.

Making the display board interactive and a tool to support learning in lessons is a theme we revisit throughout the book. Another quick and easy way is through the use of flaps that can be lifted. This display from a Year 11 tutor base (on the next page) shows where past students have gone on to study at university. The aim of the display board was to share the successes of past students and inspire others to believe that they too have the potential to achieve this. Under the mortar board is the name of the student and the course they are studying. Students are encouraged to interact with the display, and thus they learn where the different universities are and the range of courses available.

Creativity beyond the display boards . . .

In addition to the use of objects on the display boards, temporary exhibitions are also powerful. Do you remember, during science lessons, shelves filled with skulls, oversized test tubes and volcanic rock when you were at school? Writing this encouraged us to reflect on our own school experience and reminded one of us of an all-time favourite display. The winner, hands down, was the 'mouldy table'. Despite the intensifying whiff of the fur-infested feast, the 'table of mould' communicated more on the subject of decomposition than any textbook ever could. Exhibitions are memorable. Students leaving in Year 11 reminded us of exhibitions they had co-created in classrooms in Years 7 and 8. They remembered even the smallest detail – 'remember when we all bought in precious objects for our RE exhibition and you bought in a lock of your daughter's hair . . .' – and this demonstrates the power of objects to reinforce messages and learning. Using temporary exhibitions is not only quick and easy, it engages students, supports learning and is an aspect of display and environment that students can co-create. We are always struck by the enthusiasm and creativity with which students embrace this challenge, and the sense of pride and ownership it instils.

Traditionally, Science has embraced the use of temporary exhibitions. There are no reasons, however, why this cannot be extended to other areas of the curriculum and why we cannot learn lessons from this traditional practice. The English department has a table of poetry objects that relate to the subject matter of each of the poems studied. One of our favourite examples is from a Year 10 English group. Putting a Krooklok in the hands of this group after reading about a man being beaten to death could be considered risky, but this one object alone provided greater understanding for our students than any definition, also allowing the group to appreciate the horror of the violence being described. Colleagues have found using objects particularly powerful in supporting those with English as an additional language and to support the acquisition of language, but it is key in engaging all learners, and enabling access to otherwise challenging text.

We have also seen outstanding examples in primary schools. The example below from Manorside Primary appears in classrooms where Ancient Egypt is being studied. A range of images and objects linking to these topics are displayed on a table directly in front of a display board, and learners are encouraged to handle and discuss the objects that are here, bringing to life their learning.

If space is an issue, small shelves can be fitted to display boards and relevant objects can be placed on these, such as the perfume bottles shown in the Design and Technology example on the next page.

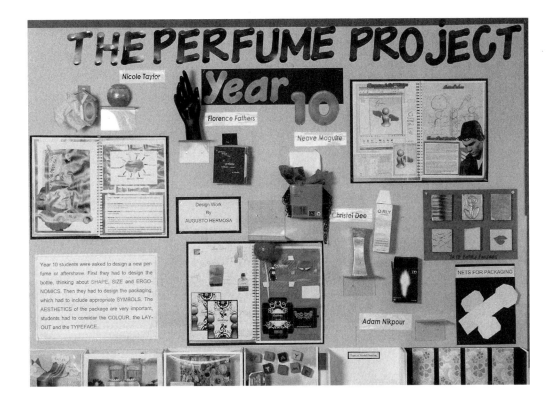

Temporary exhibitions can be set up in shared areas of the school such as the Learning Resource Centre. The example in Photograph 10 in the plate section, shows how 'fold away' boards have been set up and adorned with objects that students and staff have brought in to highlight the diversity of cultures represented at the school. This display is the focus of a learning activity and is visited by students during a cross-curricular day. 'Fold away' boards can be used to celebrate special occasions in school and/or can be set up in department offices and spaces to complement learning for a particular topic.

Using work that students have created is also a useful addition to displaying objects, and this is a great way of celebrating students' work to enhance learning. Sculptures produced by students are displayed around the school grounds. In the study of Claes Oldenburg, art students complete observational drawings of these model sculptures during the preparation stages prior to creating their own. Drawing from real models is so much more inspiring than a two-dimensional image in a book. Not only is it inspiring but it also allows the department to celebrate successful work and demonstrate what is possible; students tell us there is nothing more motivational than seeing what another student has been able to achieve and aspiring to do even better.

The same principle applies to how the Geography department uses students' project work to support the teaching of volcanoes. Past student models of erupting volcanoes are used to discuss the process of eruption and to plan creating their own models. Students' work is displayed but also used within lessons to support the learning of others. The History department does the same in creating models of the trenches, using last year's models as the classroom resource.

Spaces beyond display boards . . .

- How many display boards are there in your classroom?
- Have you enough to meet your needs?

If the answer to question 2 is 'no' then this section will offer ideas and solutions to maximize the use of all your classroom space, using space appropriately to create these exciting learning environments. In every school we visit, we see another creative example of using space beyond the display board. Teachers are brilliant at getting the very best out of their limited resources, and display space provides another good example.

We have seen examples of using the floor for display purposes. One English class arrived to discover the outline of a man on the floor of their classroom. The victim was soon identified as King Richard's brother Edward. The class had to work out from the script how he met his grisly fate. Suddenly Shakespeare was alive and kicking in their classroom (even if Edward was not!). In one classroom there are footsteps on the floor that are 'the footsteps of success', leading students to the GCSE descriptor board, and the infamous Banksy double yellow line flower from a street in London has been painted on to an Art classroom wall, running down across the classroom floor using coloured tape.

The ideas are endless and can so easily be achieved through materials such as masking tape, chalk, marker pens and pencil.

The ceiling as well as the floor can be an inspiring and original location for display, as are the windows. In Design and Technology the taste buds are studied as part of the Food Technology curriculum. Students have to identify the taste buds on different parts of the tongue using the tongue hanging from the ceiling, as can be seen in Photograph 7 in the plate section – display for learning in its truest form.

A simple, yet very effective display covers one corridor wall in the Geography department: a blown-up map below of the local area. Students are seen engaging with the map every time they are in the corridor, attempting to identify where they live, their favourite local areas and the school.

We have seen similar displays in a Science classroom, with a huge periodic table across an entire wall, and in Art, with a colour wheel painted on to the ceiling.

The Art teacher responsible for the Banksy display below wanted students to continuously question what is art, and what it is trying to communicate. To reinforce this learning the display was developed each week for a half-term with a stencilled rat appearing in a different place in the room. Students had to find where it was, say what they thought it was communicating and further explore if this was, in fact, art. This took the display beyond the constricting boards out into the classroom environment in its entirety.

Hanging cardboard boxes from the ceiling and then covering each face of the box with images, photographs or key words is also a use for this space. Unusually shaped boxes can make this interesting; we have seen this used well in Science to reinforce learning about where planets are in the solar system, and in Music with boxes hanging from the ceiling around the room to show where sections of the orchestra sit.

All well and good, but when am I going to have time?

If this is the question you have already been asking, you are not alone and we recognize that it is an important one for us to address. We explore in the leadership chapters how to give the time and resources required for a whole-school commitment to display and environment for learning, and how to work *with* workforce agreements so structures and processes are in place for teachers to plan and prepare displays, and redistribute tasks across the workforce. It is important to state here that classroom practitioners cannot change their display boards every half-term; there are simply not enough hours in the day. This chapter is about empowering and enabling you to plan and create dynamic and effective display that will serve you and your students well through a school year. Good displays are valued and appreciated by students and are easy to maintain, and therefore worthwhile investing the initial energy into. It is also important to excite your students with some changes to the classroom throughout the year and to make this process meaningful and manageable.

Hanging display out to dry

Washing lines are an excellent way to implement frequent change in the classroom. Much less time-consuming than changing display boards, the washing line becomes the moveable feast and is the only regular change that is needed. It is an effective way of displaying up-to-date student work and key words associated with the topic being taught; all you need is a ball of string and a pack of value pegs.

Simply attach a length of string from one side of the room to the other. Then, as an alternative homework task, give each student a peg and ask them to create a design on it that captures the next topic being taught. The pegs can then be used to attach model pieces of work, photographs of the students, key words, etc. to the line. Ideally work displayed on the line should be double-backed to ensure all students have access to the resource, inspiring the whole class and not only those sitting behind the washing line.

Checklist 2

- you have now been immersed in creativity
- you have explored using objects on the display board
- you have explored using objects in temporary exhibitions
- you have explored using objects produced by, and for, students
- you have explored ideas for interactivity
- you have explored using the floor, the ceilings, the walls and the windows
- we have honest about our workloads
- we have introduced the washing lines

These ideas and examples will arm you with the skills to create your own outstanding displays. The next chapter develops on this to really focus our energy on display for **learning**; how display can enhance how students learn, complement quality teaching and increase student engagement, and is packed full of more practical ideas and strategies to add to your toolkit.

Chapter 3

Display as a learning tool

However satisfying producing attractive display is, there is nothing better than when we achieve our vision for display as a learning resource and see how students' learning is enhanced by it . This chapter draws on examples of using display as a tool to support learning. These ideas are simple but effective, and most importantly they can and have been successfully used across departments and in all classrooms.

Can display really facilitate the assessment of student understanding?

The rate at which a student learns is directly affected by their ability to independently identify *what* they are learning and *how* this learning will be measured. To do this, students need to be clear about both the objective and outcome of the learning experience. Display can be used to highlight and reinforce these clear messages. At The Compton learning objectives and learning outcomes 'tiles' are simple A4 cards that are laminated and attached to the interactive whiteboard or static whiteboard in every classroom. Their purpose is twofold; not only do they act as a reminder to the teacher about the importance of sharing the aims and outcomes of the lesson, but they also allow students who may not absorb that information immediately to refer back to it during the course of the lesson if necessary. Teachers on the whole will be required to teach several different groups or subjects within one day with a short turnaround period between each lesson. If at the beginning of the lesson the teacher has not had an opportunity to write the aims and outcomes of the lesson up, a student can be selected to come up and write their interpretation of the teacher's explanation during the introductory phase. The advantage is that not only are you checking a student's understanding, but you are also engaging students to translate your explanation into student-friendly speak. Students displaying challenging behaviour can be won over by being employed as the teacher's glamorous assistant/reporter/translator.

These cards can be individualized to meet the needs of the group, in the example below the phrases 'Today I am learning about . . .' and 'I have understood it because . . .' are used.

An alternative approach is to have two large envelopes attached to your board with the objectives and outcomes in them. Students are asked at the end of the lesson to predict what the teacher had recorded as the aim of the lesson, and how they expected understanding could be measured. The originals are removed from the envelope and read to the class, and students match what they predicted with the recorded information. This is a fun and engaging way to reinforce objectives and review outcomes.

There are so many creative ways in which the learning objective and outcome cards can be used. Communicating the learning objectives as a visual display that the students then have to decode is a technique for engaging students in this important part of the lesson. Mike Fleetham[3] (education consultant, author and trainer) suggests typing lesson objectives into Word, then changing the font to Wingdings and displaying this code around the room. We have explored this using key visuals to represent each letter. Students love the decoding activity and fully engage with the lesson objective. These are displays that take minutes to prepare but are highly effective.

Each of these ideas enables the class teacher to utilize display to assess the students' understanding of the purpose of the learning. Good teachers do this with or without display, but integrating this process into the class display further enhances its importance. If students are not able to identify what the intended aim of the lesson is, it is difficult for them to see development within the lesson and how each part links to the others. If they are able to identify 'what', 'why' and 'how' through display they will value the tasks more and engage more readily. Display really can have that level of impact on the learning. Building display into the structure of the lesson enables students to value and appreciate the validity of it.

An alternative to a paper resource . . .

Display can also be used as effectively as any worksheet, card sort or video clip and can be integrated into the lesson as a central resource. The display below is used as the central focus when students are debating whether Banksy is an Artist or Vandal. The display is real: it is Banksy's work for the students to see each time they enter the room, to immerse themselves in, to consider, look at again, question and discuss. The display brings Banksy to life and enables students to use evidence in their judgements in order to build their arguments for whether this is art or vandalism. Every time they come into this classroom, their learning and previous judgements are reinforced or challenged, so that the debate lesson does not stand alone but is integrated through every visit to this classroom.

In PE the painted image of the athlete on the gym wall is used to teach the muscle groups. Again, this may be the focus of one lesson but learning is reinforced on every visit. If students want to remind themselves of previous learning they can recall the image or visit the classroom for a recap.

The Geography team created a grid reference display to support the Year 7 scheme of work on using grid references. Students are given grid references by the teachers, then practise moving the symbols on the display. This is a feature of starter, plenary and in-lesson activity, consistently reinforcing learning.

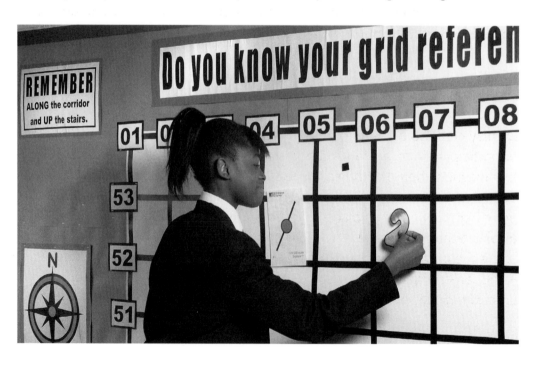

The same applies to this drama display shown in Photograph 13 in the plate section: the starter-sentence board facilitates how students evaluate performances.

An alternative to hands up . . .

Display can also be used to enable the teacher to assess who needs support. At The Compton, students' planners have a page displaying a red cross on one side and a green tick on the other, designed for students to discreetly demonstrate their understanding of a task by showing the relevant page, the cross indicating that they feel they are going to need additional help, the tick showing that they feel confident in completing the task or understand the concept. A red cross and green tick are displayed on the wall in classrooms to remind students of the purpose of the pages in the planner. See Photograph 9 in the plate section.

These symbols have been recreated across schools we work with, with smiling and sad faces, a star and wish and a plus (+) or a minus (-), with whiteboard pages in the planner where students draw the symbol to indicate understanding to their teacher. As an alternative in some schools, rather than using planners, students have a lanyard around their neck (also containing their pass) or key rings that display the symbols. In each case, the school has worked with groups of students in agreeing the symbols and the processes. The symbols are also used by staff as a tool in plenary activities to indicate whether a statement is true or false, an example of how display can be truly embedded into the review stage of the lesson.

An alternative 'who to ask?'

Display can also be used to help the teacher select students to contribute to or participate in an activity. Students' names or photographs can be attached to a magnetic board and then the teacher or a student can throw a magnetic dart to select the next contributor. Students' names can be placed on ping pong balls that are then placed in a drawstring bag that is attached to a display board with the title 'It could be you . . .': the student drawn from the bag is the next to participate. Again the ideas are endless but the principle is the same: display supports the establishment of positive relationships and crucially injects energy, fun and laughter into the classroom.

Back to hanging out the washing . . .

The photographs below and opposite show examples of washing lines, all used to actively engage students with learning and as an interactive resource. The English department has used images from *The Simpsons* to demonstrate different camera shots; a great way of engaging students who may not ordinarily be engaged. The History department used the washing line to pose the rhetorical question 'Why do we remember?' and students have to jot down their answers on the back of poppies, which are then displayed; see Photograph 14 in the plate section. In the primary school example links between washing lines are made. Flags which reflect the multicultural intake are hung in the classroom and coloured ribbons are attached for further visual impact. Key words are then hung close by and translated into the various languages as indicated by the flags. All of these examples include resources that can be removed and taken to a student's desk when required. It is a truly interactive resource that can be used to support all learners. Again display is being used as a learning tool to enhance the students' experience in the classroom.

Washing lines are great in preparing students for a new topic or idea. Ideally key words and introductory concepts should be hung from the line about a week before the topic is introduced, allowing them to subconsciously absorb the information. The introduction of new vocabulary as shown in the photograph is an ideal example of the type of resource you would display prior to the introduction of a topic. Students then start the topic familiar with some of the key vocabulary, feeling confident with the language from the start.

Level descriptors that really encourage progression

Attempting to engage students with level descriptors is a challenge; if we take on board that the key to effective display is clear, concise presentation of information it is impossible to display all level descriptors on one board. Departments which spend time and energy on simplifying level descriptors and making these student-friendly have proved that it is possible to produce clear, concise and meaningful display that students can engage with to identify where they are, where they need to be and what they need to do to get there. Using Velcro pads for this can make all the difference . . . students can remove the relevant cards, take them back to their desks and spend time identifying key skills that they need to include in the next piece of work. Departments whose level descriptors change depending on the topic taught use the Velcro pads to simply change the level descriptor cards for each topic without having to re-back and border the display time and time again.

1

2

3

4

5

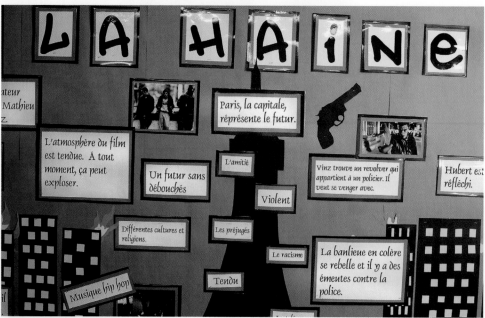

6

7

8

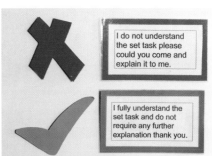

9

10

11

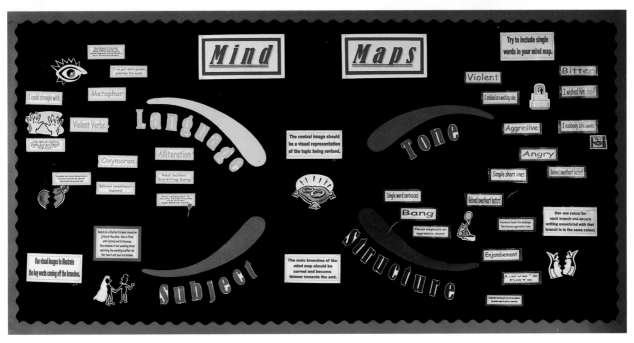

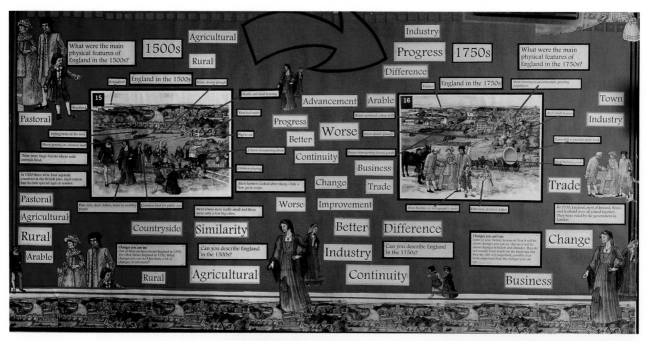

12

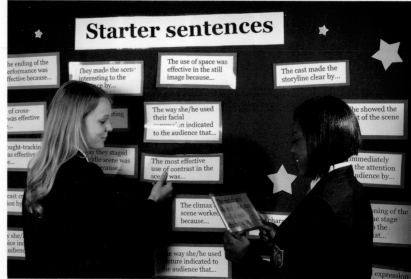

13

14

The photograph below illustrates how level descriptors can be displayed to engage students. The use of the ladder and snakes is immediately eye-catching, shows progression upwards and was co-designed by staff and students to ensure the language was appropriate. Key phrases replace the extended text from the level descriptors and key words highlight the phrase, so that rather than feeling overwhelmed, students actively engage with and use the display, using the ladder to identify the level they are at, and the necessary skills needed to progress to the next level.

In the English example overleaf the cards are attached to an ivy vine that climbs the wall. This is used as an extension task for the more able students who can identify how to further improve their work, offering teachers a personalized learning tool.

Display for all . . .

Displays that encourage students to consider the *process* of learning are also useful. Learning style displays enable students to identify which types of tasks suit their individual learning needs. The explanations are displayed on a card listing the types of activities that support specific learning styles. For example, the display board for visual learners might say: 'Visual learners learn best when they summarize information in mind-map form, they link visual images with concepts, they produce colour-coordinated summaries on Post-it notes.' Having cards up in the classroom for each possible type of learner also serves as a reminder to us as teachers, encouraging us to include a variety of tasks suitable for different learners within our classrooms. The display can also be referred to with classes revising for exams, for example 'For your homework I would like you to select the activity that will help you to revise the poem "Half Caste" most effectively: a mind map, a card sort or recording your interpretation on to your MP3 player'. A connecting display board in the classroom can then be used to model an example of one of these revision techniques. This is also useful when encouraging students to develop approaches outside their preferred learning styles. Photograph 11 in the plate section illustrates a large version of a mind map, modelling how this type of activity can be used effectively.

Checklist 3

This last section has delved deeper into the role of display as a tool to enhance learning, complement quality teaching and increase student engagement:

- you have linked your displays to learning
- you have considered how they can support a student's understanding
- you have explored alternatives to hands up
- you have looked at alternatives to selecting students to contribute
- you have revisited using the washing line
- you have looked at ways to use level descriptors
- you have considered using learning style displays

Now you are at the stage where you look at your classroom as a whole and the atmosphere you create as a teacher. This is where you put the finishing touches to creating an environment that is learning-focused, houses fantastic display and nurtures and celebrates every student that comes into it. This is your classroom, a place where you love to teach and students love to learn.

Chapter 4

What my classroom says about me as a teacher

- What does your classroom say about you and your love of teaching?
- How do students feel when they walk into your classroom?

This chapter explores beyond display boards and how you cleverly use the ceilings, floors, walls and windows. Classroom display does so much more than information sharing; fantastic display also recognizes potential, builds self-esteem, motivates and rewards all students. This goes beyond the display boards and a simple way to enhance this in your classroom is to have lots of images of successful learners: photographs of your students. Photographs show students that you care about them and that this is a place where they belong. Alongside every photograph can be a reason to celebrate an achievement. The example illustrated in the photograph Star of the Week, below, has pride of place underneath the whiteboard at the front of the classroom, celebrating students on a weekly basis, those who have met a challenge head-on and overcome it.

Positive display also encourages positive behaviour and allows students to understand that you do not focus solely on the subject you teach but also on the way in which they approach the learning of the subject. Celebrating students who have successfully overcome a challenge is a powerful reinforcement of the benefits of positive thinking; it can motivate disaffected students and those who strive to be included. Messages regarding the ethos you want to establish in the classroom can include both statements and questions that students can engage with. The display below shows expectations regarding opportunities for all. It does not dictate a message through a series of imperatives, for example, 'You will respect everyone'. Instead it encourages the students to form their own opinions by engaging with the display.

This next display example (overleaf) celebrates individual students' academic achievements and what contributed to their success. This reinforces key messages to younger students that the skills associated with success are excellent attendance, resilience, focus, carrying out research and asking questions. These displays can complement subject-specific displays and the success-focused ethos of your classroom. They also send very clear messages to students about your belief in them, your focus on learning and your expectations.

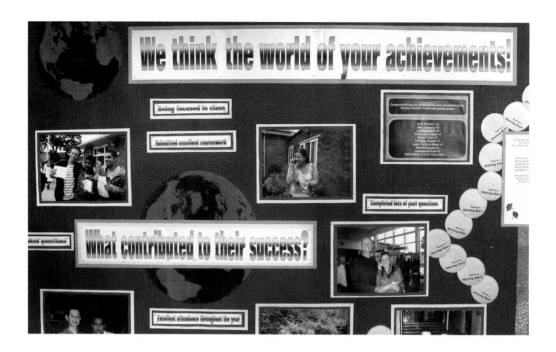

Clutter-free and orderly . . .

We were fascinated when we asked for feedback from students to the question: 'What makes a good learning environment?' They unanimously responded that they learned better in a tidy classroom, one student saying that 'chaotic classrooms equal chaotic lessons'. It is interesting that this has been the response to the student questions in each of the schools we have worked in. Students linked a tidy teacher's desk with quality lessons and good learning, and they preferred learning in classrooms where the chairs and desks were tidy and there was no rubbish. Students reported that all they could do in untidy, cluttered classrooms was spend their time re-ordering the environment in their head, rather than focusing on the task at hand.

Is my classroom conducive to learning?

A great way to determine if your classroom is conducive to learning is by putting yourself in a student's shoes, asking questions of your classroom environment from a student perspective. Sit at the back of your classroom at a student's desk and ask yourself the following sets of questions:

- Is the classroom tidy? Are desks and chairs ordered?
- What does the teacher's desk look like?
- Is it ordered and clutter-free?

Ensure that the chairs and tables are left in an orderly fashion at the end of lessons; students will respect the classroom and support you with this if there is a sense in which you take pride in your room. Build routines into the end of your lessons: chairs under, tables cleared and room tidy soon becomes a habit that shows a shared sense of ownership of the learning space, and it quickly becomes an expectation that on entering your classroom students will learn and will respect fellow learners by leaving an orderly room.

Behaviours that challenge a positive and welcoming classroom environment are not acceptable. You set the boundaries and you communicate these. This also means ensuring any graffiti disappear soon after they appear, so always have a cloth and spray to hand.

An organized classroom suggests an organized approach to classroom management and student learning, and as we ask students to present themselves and their work in an organized and orderly way, it is our responsibility in the classroom to model these behaviours, and to ensure that our classroom environment reinforces these key messages. Walls filled with celebratory quotes and smiling faces show students that this is what you expect from them!

Keeping your desk tidy can be a real challenge, but again it is about setting an expectation and a routine to enable this to be the norm. At the end of a long day, clear the decks and prepare for tomorrow; you and the students will benefit in the morning.

- Are resources that are not being used in boxes/filed away/on shelves?
- Can clutter be stored elsewhere?

Primary school teachers are generally very good at this as the curriculum requires them to teach a range of subjects in one room, so classrooms are organized with resources clearly categorized and labelled. Mouldy coffee cups, dusty books and piles of unmarked exam scripts speak volumes about how much care and attention a teacher pays to his or her classroom environment and this can directly affect a student's ability and desire to learn. For those students whose home life is chaotic, an orderly classroom environment provides security and safety, a place where they can focus and learn.

Spend time (and where necessary resources) to ensure you have storage in place, then build into your routines using this to hide away those waiting-to-be-marked scripts, the resources for future lessons and sets of textbooks. Clearly labelled storage gives the impression that you are organized, are in control of your classroom resources, and sends a powerful message to your students. Again this models the behaviours we encourage in our students.

The next questions, important to ask from a student perspective, are around the whiteboard, the central place used to communicate ideas.

- Can I read the board?
- Is it clean or is it a blur of smudges?

It is worth assessing whether or not students can read the board from all seats in the classroom, and what you can do to ensure that they can. Check whether your writing is big enough to read, as if you cannot read what is on your whiteboard, what is the point of using it? This simple assessment from a student perspective may guide how you are using the board and enable its use be maximized. We recommend owning board-cleaning fluid and a board eraser as essentials. Hide these away with your staple gun and staples!

The final questions are the most crucial. These reinforce why you have spent all your time and energy in preparing quality lessons and learning experiences, and why you have energized your displays so that they reinforce learning objectives and outcomes *and* reiterate that you believe that every child in your classroom can achieve their very best. The final questions evaluate the tone communicated in your classroom:

- Is my teacher interested in the welfare of all students in my class?
- Is there a sense that my teacher is proud of students?

And most importantly:

- Do I want to learn in this room?

What is important to students is that they enter a classroom where serious learning takes place, where their teacher means business and is motivated to ensure that all students in his or her care achieve their potential in a happy, safe and supportive environment. Students take their learning seriously when they know their teacher does too and your classroom shows everything about you as a teacher.

Checklist 4

- you have those crucial key ingredients that assert your ethos through display and beyond
- you show that your classroom is a place where all are valued and respected
- you show that your classroom is a place where all succeed and are celebrated
- you show that your classroom is a learning-focused, orderly and positive zone
- your classroom shouts that you love learning

Section 2

The School

This section moves from the classroom into the corridors and all other spaces around school. It is here that the whole-school ethos is communicated. Classroom teachers and senior leaders who are passionate about the power of display and the importance of a learning-focused environment have the ability to transform the school, communicating to every learner that they are valued and respected and that this school is where they can achieve their very best.

Through this section we maintain a focus on practical ideas and strategies by drawing on a detailed case study of developments at The Compton. This enhances your toolkit of ideas for moving display and environment for learning to new levels in your school. We emphasize the importance of leadership in developing a whole-school approach to display and environment. This section explores:

- utilizing environment to reinforce and emphasize your school ethos
- more ideas and solutions for creating dynamic and exciting corridor displays
- creative ideas for different spaces around school
- leadership and change-management strategies for developing this agenda
- staff and student engagement activities

This section of the book emphasizes the power of the wider environment to reinforce ethos, celebration, achievement and success for all. Using a detailed case study, we focus on the physical areas of school outside the classroom, not just on display boards, and importantly explore how to successfully engage staff in implementing a consistent and common approach. We share activities from a range of schools that demonstrate the power and potential of the student voice, a key feature of these processes and developments.

Chapter 5

Communicating the school ethos and culture

In our introduction we talked about initial impressions of a school and how Ofsted inspectors form an opinion within minutes of arriving in reception. To kick-start this chapter we wanted to share our first impressions of walking into Manorside Primary, where we were overwhelmed by the quality of display and the importance given to environment for learning. The Manorside example highlights the importance of these initial impressions on lasting judgements about the school and is a great way to celebrate this school as a shining example of what is possible.

We walked into their reception and entered a world where a love of learning dominates. There are children's faces beaming at you from every angle: Tung Ching welcomes you in Mandarin, Joe is standing, looking in awe at his framed macaroni Van Gogh masterpiece and Jessica in Year 5 draws your attention to the 'trips and activities photo book' on the visitors' table. The learning and achievement culture permeates everything you can see, hear and touch; you enter the Manorside community, their belief system, their vision and you feel proud to be part of it and proud of what is being achieved.

Sanctuary in the making . . .

The reception area offers the first taste of your school culture and a great starting place is to ask yourself the questions:

- What is the first impression we *create* of our school? and then
- What is the first impression we *want to create* of our school?

A useful activity is to carry out a 'display walk' of the reception area (and vicinity) to capture initial thoughts. This can be done with groups of students and staff (and if you are feeling brave, with a group of parents). Digital and video cameras are a powerful way of capturing what you see and focusing discussion. This discussion can lead to agreeing how the reception area can and should be used to display key messages about the school and an action plan to enable this to happen.

What are the school's core values and beliefs?

How to display the school's core values and beliefs *and* present a sense of the school's long-term vision is an important consideration in the reception and welcome area of the school. Displaying the school mission statement or motto is particularly powerful as these are so often now produced, agreed and developed by *all* those in the school community and reflect the culture of the school. The values of the school can be consolidated into one statement that captures the ethos of the school. The example below, Learning Together, Achieving Success communicates so much more than the four words on the wall. It suggests a shared ethos, a positive approach, a belief in every student, high expectations and success for all. Students, staff, parents and visitors are welcomed into a school where this is the culture.

Many schools display mission statements or mottos in different languages to represent the diversity of the school community. This simple approach is inclusive and welcoming, especially when signs can be accessed by all in the school community. Building on the Manorside example above, a reception area that is welcoming, vibrant and positive enhances any ethos statement and shows *evidence* that this is the case. At The Compton, large photographs of happy students and vibrant displays of student art work welcome students, staff and visitors. There are well-maintained plants and the entrance area is kept clean and tidy. Display boards reflect achievement, successes and celebration, and the impression created is that this is a school that cares about its students and staff and has a focus on achievement and success.

Communicating your ethos

The examples below draw from ones we have seen in many schools. In revisiting how your reception area communicates your school's core values and beliefs, it may be worth including in your planning a process for reviewing and enhancing these:

- Display photos of happy learners, a point we have reiterated through the book. Happy learners suggest happy experiences. Consider your home: you will probably have images of loved ones throughout your house. It is no different in school; celebrate the fact that you care about your students. Photographs are a cheap and highly effective way of creating positive display and enhancing your environment. Hire a photographer and invite them to school for one or two days, and work beforehand with department teams to find out what activities they think will be represented well through photographs. Plan a timeline for the photographer's time with you, aiming to capture the ethos of each department and the school through photographs. Once finished, these photographs can be printed as boards and displayed around school. These images show inspirational teaching and positive working relationships in the school, reinforcing the school's ethos *and* providing great display.
- Share recent positive newspaper coverage of the school and local or national recognition of particular achievements, displayed in frames and/or as a display board. Responsibility for these displays can lie with talented non-teaching staff (as explored in the leadership section below).

- Framed certificates highlight the school's strengths and achievements. Many schools display their certificates and this sends a very clear message that the school celebrates achievement. Parents and visitors to the school can share in this culture and hard-working staff are recognized. Recognition encourages and motivates students and has the same effect on adults.

- Visitors should wait in an area that feels calm and relaxed. At The Compton, the visitors' space is painted blue, a colour associated with feelings of tranquillity. A small screen also features in the waiting room and displays the focus for the week. Money has been invested in furniture that creates a specific welcoming feel. Having reading materials such as the school prospectus, school newsletter, school magazine and other publications available further promotes the positive culture of the school. Visitors are provided with display to look at and publications to read that reinforce all the positives associated with the school. Sitting in a calm environment is a positive welcome to the school.
- Show how much pride you take in the work that students produce; display quality work that communicates that high-quality teaching and learning take place and that the school has high expectations of its students. In the photograph on the next page both Art and Design and Technology work is displayed in glass cabinets, giving visitors an insight into the types of projects students engage with.

- Many schools now use a parent/visitor voice box, and displaying this in the reception area reinforces the understanding that the views of parents and visitors are important to you. Providing a tick-box questionnaire that can be filled in while they wait in the reception area enables you to glean more feedback from your parents and visitors when they have time to do it. The questions can be tailored to meet the needs of your school and can include feedback on uniform, behaviour, noise levels, etc. and can vary according to any areas you are keen to focus on.

- Alder Grange School in Rossendale displays 'You said, we did . . .' in reception to show what has happened as a result of acting on parental feedback. This further encourages the wider community to engage with the school and reinforces the message that everyone in the school community is valued and listened to.

- Including a space for visitors to comment on the welcome they have received, as part of the signing-in process, provides positive feedback and clear direction if there are areas that need development. Again it reinforces to visitors that they are welcome and that their views and input are important.

- Another example is a board in the reception area where students have been invited to write on cards reasons why they are proud of their school. The display board 'We are proud of our school because . . .' provides parents with an insight into how students view their school, reinforcing positive messages about the school, the students and the school culture.

Communicating your ethos through display

The same principles apply in creating quality displays on boards in reception and around school. 'It's all in the planning . . .' is a useful beginning point whether your display is subject-specific or a celebration board.

Outstanding display in shared areas multitasks, it improves the appearance of the environment, it encourages positive relationships, raises self-esteem and celebrates student success. If the environment mirrors respect and care, learners feel respected and cared for and this can be felt by visitors too. Within the reception area visitors are exposed to success and celebration and achievement; utilizing display boards across the school is an opportunity to echo this.

Chapter 6

The Compton School case study: celebrating achievement – the ghost children as well as the Mars bar kids

Display is a very powerful way of ensuring that all children are recognized, celebrated and valued, and this is an opportunity to be seized through displays in your communal areas. Children are diverse and that is what makes our job so interesting, so utilizing display to recognize and celebrate all students is core to the development of the display policy.

At The Compton we agreed that there are traditionally two types of learners: firstly, the 'ghost children', those who come into school on time, dressed in perfect uniform, arrive to lessons on time, complete the work, are not necessarily academically gifted and then go home to complete their homework. Are these the children that are ardently discussed in your staffroom at the end of the day? No.

Those discussed are the 'Mars bar kids', those who are so disruptive that when they do allow teachers to teach they are rewarded by a very grateful teacher with a metaphorical bar of chocolate. What does that teach our students?

We initiated a significant cultural shift so that the critical mass of delightful young people are acknowledged, and the child who always behaves and always tries is the one who features in celebrating achievement displays in the corridor. There are no ghost children, successful learning at all levels is taught and celebrated and all colleagues have bought into this through some of the processes explored in the leadership chapter below. Appendix 1 shows the achievement board policy.

Each term every department in the school identifies eight to 12 students who have achieved within the department area. The students' photographs and a summary of their achievements are displayed in the department corridor. Our initial fears that students would not like their photographs being displayed were immediately alleviated as students across the year groups were delighted when they saw that they were being recognized, and they have fed back that it is highly motivational and they strive to be included on the board. In a student questionnaire 80 per cent confirmed that they feature in a display within school and 96 per cent said they wanted to be featured. In addition to students feeling included, teachers can also see a variety of students across the curriculum being celebrated. It offers an alternative perspective on a child: a child who may not be doing well in one area can excel in another and this can help to alter expectations of that child. The first example of an achievement board celebrates the 'amazing progress of students of all abilities'. The focus is on students' GCSE results from the previous year, comparing their actual result with data from the Fischer Family Trust (FFT) which estimates their expected rate of progress (based on the progress of similar pupils in similar schools nationally in previous years).[4] This is also mirrored in the ICT board example that celebrates students within the department. The students displayed range from those predicted an E through to those predicted an A*. All students feel comfortable because it is the effort and rate of progress that is celebrated.

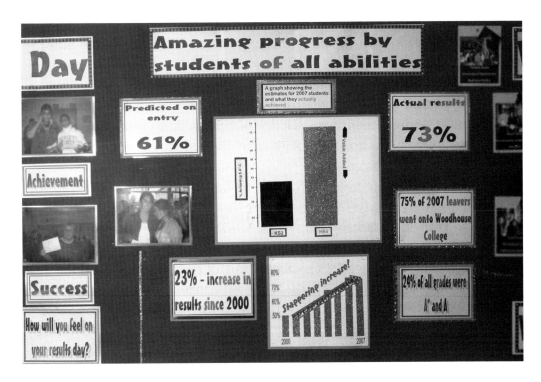

In the example below, being able to speak two languages is celebrated, alongside many other achievements and skills the students have.

This photograph illustrates the 'honours board' created as part of a rewards scheme. This is a high-profile display on the main wall of the central communal area. The categories recognize students with a diverse range of skills and talents, showing that, across the school, all talent and skills are celebrated and rewarded, and all students are encouraged to engage with the reward system, knowing they will be recognized and celebrated for their talents and strengths. The photograph shows the different categories: academic achievement and progress, contribution to extracurricular activities, contribution to the life of the school, the Andrew Macalpine Award for boys' achievement and the Governors' Award for girls' achievement.

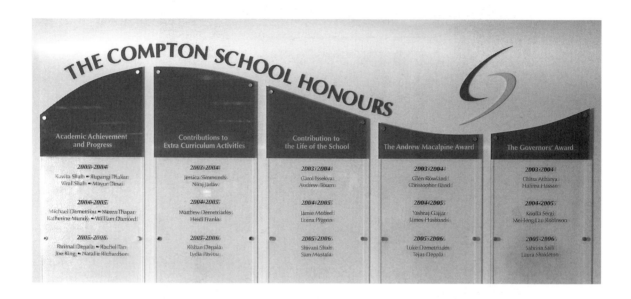

The power of language . . .

Although images play a crucial role in communicating a school philosophy, language does too. One place to begin the display improvement journey is by looking at signage and the power of positive language in serving the school ethos. The first change made was to the rather direct poster 'Put litter in the bin'. it was agreed that it should read: 'We respect our environment and put litter in the bin.' Including the pronoun 'we' and the positive reinforcement of 'respect' immediately encourages the school approach and ethos to be communicated to students, staff, parents and visitors. A powerful factor here was the students' leadership role. This was developed further by the student council, who wrote the summarized version of the mission statement. The original aims included: 'We aim to encourage each student to become a positive member of the community.' Students felt this was too wordy and suggested 'We are all positive members of the community.'

Removing the word 'student' and replacing it with 'all' instantly suggests the school is a community rather than two disparate groups. Students then led on a display project that involved collecting quotes that inspired them. These were matched with images of the students and then the quotes and images were put in high-quality frames and placed along one of the stairwells. The examples in this photograph read:

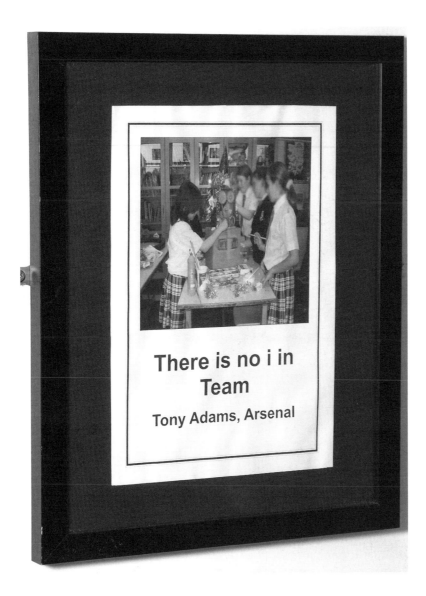

'Aiming high, achieving high.'

'I am always doing that which I cannot do, in order that I may learn to do it.' Pablo Picasso

'There is no "i" in team.' Tony Adams

'Whenever you learn something new the whole world becomes much richer.'

This approach influenced signage across the school, permeating through to staff who began to create individualized signs to support the embedding of school policy. This was the approach used by one member of staff to remind students about having their planner out on the desk. The use of 'please' completely changes the tone and the sign acts as a positive reminder rather than a command.

Please remember to have your planner open on your desk

This principle is also used when embedding policy with staff. The momentum of the rewards system was sustained with regular, supportive and encouraging reminders regarding the policy. Language was carefully selected and the justification for issuing credits was the focus.

When students do all that is asked of them in a lesson and sound learning has taken place as a result, please remember to reward them with a credit. Thank you

As a result of the success of the work around the language and use of signage, the home and school contract, school rules and day-to-day language of the school, including that on the classroom door, has been reviewed and amended, with students and staff leading developments.

Don't close the door and become self-employed

Display at The Compton is as much about creating a learning culture as it is about displaying material that will enhance understanding of a topic. An example of this is the use of a positive statement on the doors of classrooms. For us, removing teachers' names from classroom doors was a good first step, reaffirming that we are a community, with shared responsibility for and ownership of all our spaces; each classroom is a shared learning area, and the teacher is responsible for creating and enabling a learning zone. The signs used in and around school, and the messages that signage and display deliver, are key in ensuring a learning-focused climate. The use of a positive statement on the door of the classroom – 'You are about to enter a learning environment' or 'Welcome to Geography, the world awaits you' – encourages students to enter a zone that is positive and will challenge them; an environment where the tone and teachers' expectations for the lesson are set. It speaks volumes about the shared common ethos, mutual respect and inclusive ownership of learning expectations.

The classroom door is another opportunity to communicate celebratory messages. The recognition of musical talent in the music department is a model example of this: 'It is your talent that makes this department so special.' This conveys to students that this is a learning community of which they are a crucial member.

Policy into practice through display . . .

In addition to setting the tone, display can also be utilized to embed whole-school policy. This has included whole-school approaches to seating plans, positive behaviour, celebrating achievement and wearing the school uniform correctly.

Seating plans were introduced to improve standards of teaching and learning and to support embedding this as consistent policy each classroom displayed the seating plan for each half-term. This was very powerful in challenging the initial 'But I don't want to sit with her, I learn better with my mate, Miss.' Students found the same display in every classroom and the same practice from every teacher. Students were in seating plans in every lesson and the rationale for doing so was clearly articulated through a focus on improving learning.

Once embedded, students were asked why they thought seating plans had been introduced and their responses were added to the displayed seating plans, further reinforcing the rationale behind them. Examples include: 'To encourage us to work with a range of people' and 'To support us to behave so we can learn best'. Displaying them on the wall gives the seating plan validity and encourages a prompt, calm start to the lesson that is consistently implemented by all.

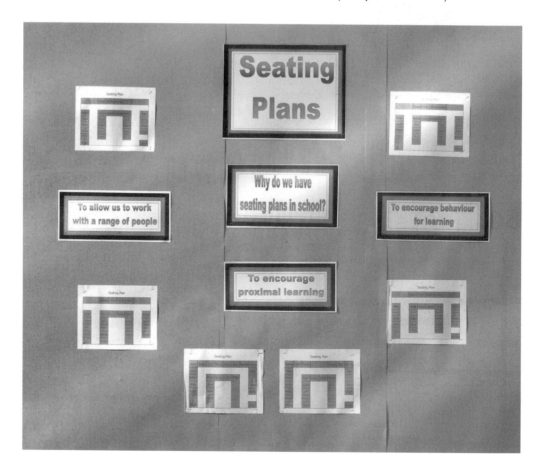

Transforming uniform through display: a big bag of carrots and a very small stick

Display is now a key feature of any cultural shift and change at The Compton; no magic wands or radical initiatives; just good old consistency and loads of positive reinforcement. Display has enabled this to be a whole staff approach, not just senior leaders walking the corridors or popping in and out of classrooms. Display has empowered others to challenge what had previously been accepted and continues to do so.

The uniform launch was introduced with displays of different tie knots. Boys really bought into the 'Windsor knot culture' and began to believe that dressing like a man was something to aspire to rather than the previously popular *Hollyoaks* culture that had prevailed. Once key players began to dress differently and take pride in their appearance, photographs of them were taken and displayed on the plasma screen with the quote 'I wear my uniform correctly because . . .' This is highlighted in the top left-hand corner of the image below of the reception area.

During the uniform launch, ideas were gathered from students: 'Why as a school are we focusing on uniform?' These were added to the display so that powerful messages about the reasons behind uniform were explained to students, by students themselves. As a result of this approach students began to change their perceptions, saying that they understood why it should be a priority, that it showed a sense of pride in themselves and their school and that they had chosen the uniform. Cinema trips for the best dressed and bottles of champagne for the tutors with the smartest tutor group have also been popular incentives. But predominantly it is down to the public communication of a message via display that supported the change.

Twenty-first-century learning

The final stage in developing display at The Compton was to consider how we use it to motivate and engage the twenty-first-century student.

Using flat screens as a tool within the learning environment has become increasingly popular in schools. Positive images and statements on a rolling display in the entrance hall, dining rooms and around school promote the school ethos and reinforce key messages to staff, students and visitors to the school. Plasma displays celebrate students who have achieved outstanding effort in their reports; students are not identified according to academic ability but the effort put into their studies. These students' names run as ticker tape across the bottom of the screen, congratulating them for being positive and successful learners. Also on display are positive messages of encouragement for students entering the hall on exam days, including images of students working hard with core messages such as 'your hard work will pay off'. One teacher displayed photographs of students when they were at primary school with images of them in their final year with their FFT estimates and what she believed they could achieve. This was shown on the plasma screen just prior to them entering their GCSE exam, encapsulating the power of belief: the students knew that they could achieve their very best and that their teacher was proud of them, and there was not a dry eye in house! The school uses digital images at every opportunity both to celebrate and motivate but also to embed whole-school practices.

Ideas and strategies – a summary

● Use photographs across the schools: images of happy learners reinforce this message and are a cheap and highly effective way of using space. This is a great tool to support staff with corridor displays.

- Use display to reinforce ethos statements and to emphasize the school's core values and principles and commitment to learning.
- Use display to reinforce key school policies, highlighting the rationale behind it and making the links to the school ethos. Longdean School, Hertfordshire has raised attendance figures by using display to reinforce messages about why good attendance is important and the links between good attendance and achievement. Every child's attendance figure is displayed and updated and those with 100 per cent attendance are celebrated. These messages are reinforced through all communication between the school and home and through the school's positive local profile.
- Use display to celebrate *every* achievement in the school, from a positive profile for the school in a local paper, to how many students participated in sports day. Bartley Green School, Birmingham displays the percentage of A* to C grades achieved by the school in every corridor, on every window and on every door, constantly reinforcing the message that every child achieves at the school. Every student can articulate that the school has high expectations of them and that the teaching, learning and support means they will achieve beyond their expected grades.
- Show pride in the quality work your students produce: display it in cabinets, as stand-alones or hanging displays.
- Let your reception and welcome area broadcast your celebration of achievement and focus on success.
- Use signage to positively reinforce your ethos.
- Utilize classroom doors to reinforce messages about learning.

Chapter 7

Leading change

Experience has led us to generalize that, in every school, teachers tend to sit in one of three camps regarding display. The first includes those who are sent into a frenzied state of panic at the sound of a staple gun; the 'I just can't do it' gang. The second are those who see display as a chore, an onerous task that has to be done but as quickly and infrequently as is possible; the 'leave display up until it meets a tragic sun-bleached death' gang. And the third, in contrast, are those who transform their classroom into a Moroccan souk, an Amazonian jungle or the Moon; a hive of learning activity captured through display that extends way beyond the standard boards placed in most classrooms. These colleagues, the 'every child matters, every display matters' gang, celebrate the fact that display is a key factor in creating a positive learning climate. They prioritize the importance of display, and have moved beyond simply seeing it as 'another thing to do' to seeing it as a liberating tool for learning, cementing the ethos of celebration and success that is a feature of their teaching. This 'gang' may not even be artistic but they are creative in the ways they inspire their students and recognize the power of the environment in supporting this ethos. These good and outstanding teachers spend time writing lesson plans and preparing materials with clear objectives and outcomes, to motivate and excite their students, and do not lead them to a drab room void of energy or care. Tthey see that display is as crucial as the lesson preparation itself; they value display as an intrinsic part of the lesson preparation.

School leaders have a responsibility to nurture and celebrate the 'every child matters, every display matters' gang but also to acknowledge the genuine concerns and fears of the others. The 'I just can't do it' and 'leave display up until it meets a tragic sun-bleached death' gangs will rightly quote that under workforce agreements display is one of the identified tasks that teachers are told not to undertake. The challenge is working with these colleagues in recognizing that display and environment is so much more than an admin task. This can be done and these points are well worth exploring:

● provide time and resource to upskill and build confidence with display

- ensure time and resources are invested in moving towards a shared, common approach and ethos, that display and environment matter, make a difference and are a priority
- ensure this time and resources are deployed for the engagement of the whole school community
- provide practical and administrative support from talented non-teaching colleagues

The challenge is to find creative approaches to staffing and resource deployment so that teaching staff are enabled to deliver high-quality learning experiences with and for students (complemented by outstanding display), supported by talented and committed non-teaching colleagues.

Effective leadership will encourage all staff to join the 'every child matters, every display matters' gang, and distributed and sustainable leadership will keep display and environment as an ever-evolving, developing agenda; meeting this challenge is achievable and rewarding, and the carrot lies firmly with the potential of environment and display to impact on learning, engagement and achievement.

Getting staff on board . . .

The strategies and processes explored here are specific to developing a whole-school approach and ethos with display and environments for learning, in encouraging whole-school cohesion, whole-school consistency and, most importantly of all, whole-school belief. These are, however, common to planning and implementing whole-school change. Readers committed and passionate about this agenda, with years of experience with change management, as well as those new to it, may glean ideas that can be tweaked, developed and adapted to suit your school's specific need and uniqueness, but common to us all is the need to bring staff together.

These three examples demonstrate how different schools have approached the challenge:

In example one, the senior team agreed that refocusing display and environment as a tool for learning needed to be a high priority, as part of the next stage in developing their whole-school teaching and learning policy. The senior team knew that there would be some opposition to this, so the initial staff meeting was seen as crucial in giving these staff an opportunity to be honest about the challenges. During a staff meeting that focused on teaching and learning an activity was introduced to explore barriers to effective teaching and learning. As part of this activity, staff were asked to list on Post-it notes all the reasons why display was challenging. Staff were split into non-departmental teams and each group was given one focus, their task to find solutions to barriers/challenges. One of these groups focused on finding solutions to the challenges of display. The senior team took this feedback and developed a whole-school, solution-focused approach to display and environment for learning. At the next staff meeting feedback from each barrier/challenge activity was presented to staff, so that the display work was already embedded within a wider focus on further developing teaching and learning. Staff concerns and worries were addressed head-on as a series of solutions, the senior team were seen to be supporting development with resources and time, and the carrot was further improving teaching and learning. It was positively received by the staff.

In example two, the senior team presented a desire to develop display and environment for *learning* as a priority for the next academic year. Images from around the school were shown, championing quality displays and showcasing areas of the school that reinforced ethos messages and celebrated success and achievement. In groups, staff were asked to list their top ten tips for quality classroom display (based on their experience and from the images they had seen); these were collated and passed to heads of department for the next team meeting. Each team was asked to produce department-specific topic sheets and a list of ideas and themes that lend themselves to effective display. The head of department was asked to use this to create a personalized department checklist to support the preparation of display. An example from the History and RE departments is included as Appendix 2.

These lists were taken to a middle management meeting and a centralized display policy was created, setting high expectations for display in every department and for every corridor display board. A student focus group was asked to review the list and develop this to include expectations for the school environment. This included taking the policy to every tutor group for input and development. The resulting policy was a practical guide to producing quality display, with an ethos statement about why the school was committed to developing display and environment for learning. The development of this policy and action is a feature of the school's ongoing plan.

In example three, student, staff and parent groups completed an audit of the school environment, exploring a range of questions about classroom and corridor displays, the reception area, the school grounds, the toilets and communal areas. Each group was asked to collate their findings and feedback to a staff meeting: what was good and what needed improving. From these presentations, in groups staff agreed a common ethos, set of actions and their desires for a development plan. This triggered visits to other schools, a review of resource allocation and the three original groups coming together with the senior team to write a three-year development plan. Staff, students and parents led the audit, all staff contributed to the future vision, and a detailed thorough development plan was the outcome of this work over which the school community had ownership.

But time is so precious . . .

Despite the different approaches used in the above examples to *launch* a focus on display and environments, how this is followed up and actioned is common across the three. Staff are given both *time* and *resources* in order to put their action plans in place – this is the priority given to the agenda by the senior leadership team.

Dedicating meeting and INSET time to developing displays is key. This can be built into the year plan; in these examples, a significant development period with more than one meeting slot allocated was used to kick-start developments, with 'top-up' time built in later in the year. 'Top-up' time is made up of sections of department/pastoral meetings dedicated to the development of this work. At The Compton, the expectation is that class and corridor display boards are replaced yearly if the display is still in excellent condition, a great incentive to ensure it is put up securely and maintained. Washing lines are replaced half-termly and time is provided through department and team meetings. Support teams and resources are provided to assist teachers at the time of replacing washing lines. A top tip here is to provide pizza. The pizza itself is insignificant (although staff love it). What is being communicated is all-powerful, that we value and respect that staff are working hard on displays and the environment. Display-focused meetings are now often associated with pizza and staff have come to look forward to this as a treat.

We have included below ideas for utilizing meeting time. These have been used in both primaries and secondaries; the major difference is the number of staff a primary school can deploy for support, and the number of colleagues who can form the 'expert' or 'champion' groups. Despite the difference in number of staff, these examples have been used to positive effect and may be worth exploring with your staff:

- Find out who your non-teaching display 'champions' are, and include these colleagues in all your training and development activity.
- Creatively assess how many resources you can provide for this development, and create a resource bank (card, staples, borders, laminator, etc.) that your 'champions' can rely on.
- Ask staff to nominate a classroom or display board that is in need of a facelift, and allocate a team of 'champions' to this room/board during an allocated meeting slot. Each team has to complete a 'changing rooms' transformation to the room/board within the allocated time. Resources and materials are prepared in advance by your nominated non-teaching 'champion' or team of 'champions'.
- Provide a group of students with a curriculum overview for each subject for the following term. Students must come up with an object or key visual for each subject. One object or image is randomly selected from a bag or pillowcase by one colleague from each department/team, and their team are then responsible for creating a display around this object/image.
- Give staff notice that the next team meeting is dedicated to updating/producing display, and if staff choose to complete this another time they can use the meeting slot to go home early.

An important message here is to strike while the iron is hot. While staff are clear on the rationale and reasons behind the development, and are enthusiastic about its potential impact on learning, get the process started with a staff meeting. Other top tips and ideas have evolved from the work we are doing at The Compton and across other schools, and some of these may be appropriate to your school:

- Appoint a member of the senior team who is absolutely committed to lead on developments with display and environment.
- Include display and environment for learning responsibilities in job descriptions.
- Include these as a target for performance management (this can link to the cycle of observations that we explore below).
- Encourage your advocates to work as a group to 'champion' the power of display as a learning tool, and have department 'champions' on hand to support other colleagues; these can be teaching or non-teaching staff (or in some cases students).
- Audit your school community for volunteer 'display champions'. You will have talented parents and school supporters who will offer time to support with display and/or environment – the challenge is finding them. We have seen stunning murals, a sculpture park and exhibitions

produced by parent-led teams, and active parent groups producing corridor and classroom displays alongside staff and students.

- Set up focus groups to specialize in different areas of this agenda, for example a group to research the impact of display on learning in your school, then a group or groups to support producing display, for example a 'putting up a display' expert group, and a 'consultation' or 'display support' group.

- Set up focus fortnights (or weeks) when all meetings are cancelled to give staff time to refresh or enhance display (this is useful to do when the washing lines are due to be replaced). The 'champions' can have resources well stocked and can also be given preparation time.

- Build all developments into the school calendar. This enables staff to see that it is given high priority, is planned for and that they can prepare through their lesson planning and preparation. It encourages staff to always look for new and exciting ways of developing their displays.

- Build feedback on classroom environment through lesson observations. This empowers all colleagues involved in observation to have ownership over the expectations for classroom environment, and allows these colleagues to showcase the excellent examples they are seeing and/or to mobilize support if it is required. It maintains that display and environment are integral to high-quality teaching and learning. The questions asked in Chapter 4 may be a useful guide here.

- Keep a photograph archive of previously successful display. This can be used for future staff development activity and provides a benchmark across the school and within departments and teams. It can also be used as a tool with students, to explore answers to questions: how could this display have supported learning? Or how could this display be improved to support learning, etc.

- Build into the calendar display 'walkabouts' and/or have ad hoc ones. This can involve staff and students (and, if you are brave, parents) to review what is going well and what could make it even better. These can be as short as fifteen minutes or can be set up as a review, then a meeting to prepare feedback for staff. These work well in schools that have made significant progress with their work.

- Create videos of students using displays to enhance learning. These can be shared with parents at events and/or through the school website, shared with staff to reinforce key messages about why display is so important, used for new staff induction and training and used as a training tool to further develop practice.

- Be proactive in preparing for developments with display on a practical level. Do any departments have a disproportionate number of corridor display boards and will that unfairly impinge on workload for that department in comparison to others? It may be worth removing some of the boards and replacing them with large photographs of students (preferably engaged in an activity that is relevant to that department). Forward planning to ensure there is, as far as possible, equality in workload will enable staff to want to engage with new developments.

These examples show what can be done and what is possible in developing display and environment for learning policies and ensuring that these are consistently applied in practice. It is relatively easy for a senior team to write a good policy on display and proudly file this under 'done'; the challenge is taking the commitment and translating this so that every class, every corridor and every communal area reflects the school ethos through displays, images, statements, pictures, photographs, the list goes on . . . We have debated whether or not to include an example of a thorough display policy in the book. The discussion centres around whether this can be enabling, or whether it could be disempowering. For colleagues who are passionate about co-creating a display policy, they will get it right. It will be unique to their school, it will engage the whole school community in its development and it is likely that it will be consistently implemented so that all staff and students reap the benefits. Further development will be built into ongoing action plans and our providing a template policy is unnecessary.

But then . . . starting from scratch can be daunting and an existing policy that has been consistently implemented can provide a framework to guide discussions; it may kick-start the planning and delivery process; it can provide peer support ('this is possible . . .') and the end result can still be a meaningful policy that translates into action and positive change. We concluded that we would have wanted to read such a policy before we began our work on display, and that many of the schools we work with find it a useful tool. The Compton policies are included as Appendix 3.

To summarize, developing an effective display and environment for learning policy needs to include the whole school community. The ideas and strategies above are underpinned by the principle that distributing leadership leads to policy that is unique and appropriate to the school, owned and supported by all, sustained and developed by all and is therefore effective. This chapter has explored distributed leadership across *all* staff in the school; the following chapter explores one of the most powerful tools available to school leaders to enable culture shift: distributing leadership through student voice.

Chapter 8

Distributing leadership – student voice

A section on leading whole-school change is incomplete without including the most important members of the school community, the students. Through all our activity around display and environment we have found working with student groups the most rewarding, challenging (in a positive way) and outcome-heavy. Where schools work with their student community, learn from their feedback and engage students fully in the leadership for change processes, the results have been significant. In response to a common question, 'How can we get students to value display and the school environment?' the key is ownership. These points are as obvious as our list of positives and negatives at the very start of the book. Our motivation for sharing the ideas we have developed, or seen in other schools, is that every time we see or share something it grows into something bigger and better. As we say above, for every idea you see here, you will have ten of your own and these ideas make a real difference.

- Create a working group of students to produce a questionnaire to find out what others feel about display and the environment; use the school council or an existing student group to share the questionnaire across the school, collate feedback and share findings from the questionnaire with the senior or middle leadership team and/or governors. From the findings the group can propose developments and action points that can lead development activities with staff.
- Other working groups can focus on a specific area of display and environment. Groups of students can design the school's mission statement board and the school's logo, which gives them ownership over key features of their school. The logo and mission statement are displayed in every area of the school, reinforcing the message that these are student-designed and that students in this school co-construct developments.
- Enable students to contribute to key displays in communal areas. Ask students to write statements about what their school means to them. Display these statements in corridors and communal areas.

Schools with specialist status can ask students to say what this means to them. These statements can be used across the school to celebrate the school's status; this is what technology means to me . . .; this is what being a specialist arts college means to me . . . Having student feedback as the basis of these displays further enhances their sense of ownership and belonging.

- Allowing secondary students to return to their primary school with a video camera, capture their favourite learning environments and produce a presentation explaining why they remember this environment so fondly, can kick-start an action or development plan in the secondary school.

- Alternatively, partnering up with a local school and running an exchange visit to share what is great, and what needs development, is a way for students to see what is positive about their own school, and use examples from another school to drive forward action planning and development.

- The audit technique can be used with a specific focus; for example we worked with a group of students across three schools in looking at how they used signage. Visiting students were able to demonstrate where the signage made sense or didn't, in finding their way around, and recommend ways that this could be improved or developed. Across the schools, students reviewed whether the signs reflected an ethos of being inclusive. Their recommendations meant the signs changed from being top-down– 'put learning first' – to inclusive – 'we put learning first'. Students requested that signs saying 'staff only, no students' were changed to 'staff relaxation zone' or similar; this also gave staff and students the opportunity to discuss why staff needed quiet time in the staffroom, and the students became advocates of protecting this quiet time and working with other students to respect it.

- At St John the Baptist School, Woking a student group presents a display 'Oscar' each term to a member of staff whose classroom environment is outstanding. This student group visits every classroom to see which ones enable and support learning and have fantastic displays, and the group gives feedback on why the member of staff has won the award.

- Engaging students as researchers can further support areas of the development plan. Interviewing other students and staff about why display is important and how it can impact on learning, can produce a powerful piece of action research to support whole-school development with display and environment.

- Have an email account set up where students can feed back any issues they have seen with the environment: if a lock is broken in a toilet, if the drain is overflowing, graffiti has appeared, etc. At St John the Baptist school, this group are called the Stars and they closely monitor emails to ensure prompt action. Encourage students to feed back positives and things to celebrate here as well.

- Work with students in existing groups and clubs to look at the school environment. The Art club can take responsibility for creating a mural on an ugly wall; the Textiles club can produce an unusual storage cover; the Maths club can produce facts and figures for specific displays.
- Specific student groups can become 'experts' with display: the 'colour coordination consultants', the 'get my display board ready' group and the 'display champions' can all support and enable staff with their work and become advocates among the student community. These can reflect the specific expertise and requirements of your school.

Honest feedback means setting the direction . . .

Presenting honest feedback to staff about what students feel about the school environment and the displays can be powerful and is a technique that can be used in staff meetings at whatever stage you are in this development process. When staff have worked so hard with displays, showing them honest feedback from the students who value the displays, and who make connections about how these are helping them learn and enjoy their lessons, has proved highly motivational (and a very good way to introduce the next development area . . .)

Will students please come to the diary room?

We learned a very useful approach to glean honest, constructive and focused feedback from students. Mike Fleetham calls this 'the *Big Brother* diary room experience' and you will immediately see that it has many different uses. Mike suggests setting up a room where students can respond to a camera without being interrupted and without having a member of staff present. Questions are taped to the wall, such as 'The most memorable display in school is . . .', 'Rooms I find it most difficult to work in are . . .', etc. A member of staff explains to the group of students how to turn the camera on and off, and may even demonstrate how they might answer one question; this includes running through basic rules such as not naming and shaming, honest and fair feedback, etc. Students are then left to offer their opinions, without a member of staff present. This is powerful as students can talk freely, consider their responses and are not influenced by anyone else. These opinions can be collated and provided to staff, to form the start of a discussion or to celebrate recent development. Alternatively, and arguably more powerful, is to edit the responses and show them at the staff meeting. Staff are generally very receptive to this, as rather than a dictated, top-down change, students are offering honest feedback about how they learn best and what can be done to improve this. A challenging student sharing that they focus better in well-maintained classrooms can in some cases be motivation enough. How can staff not engage with such powerful feedback? This is how we can learn even better.

Conclusion

Whether in your classroom or across your school, getting display right, and creating environments conducive to learning, will enhance the experiences of all in your school community. Teresa Tunnadine, Headteacher at The Compton, emphasizes the school's commitment to this:

> Seeing the impact positive display has on childrens' participation in school is a key motivator to make sure our learning environment is as good as it can be. In our school we constantly ask the following questions:
>
> ● What does excellent practice look like?
> ● Have we provided staff with sufficient time, resources and training to achieve these high standards?
> ● Are staff clear on why we need excellent display and how this impacts positively on learning and behaviour?
>
> Display and a wider commitment to a positive learning environment is not just something that the Art department does well, it is something that all can and should be involved in. At The Compton, staff are encouraged to look at each other's work, to gain ideas and to see excellence first hand. Outstanding work is spotted and rewarded with cards and comments. This keeps display high profile. There is a sense of professional pride in wanting to do it well and in recognizing why it is so important.
>
> Our CPD programme revisits display annually. This helps to emphasize its importance and keeps us all highly skilled. We also provide high-quality materials at no expense to departments to help us produce the most professional looking displays possible – sugar paper is banned here!
>
> We also make a point of spotting those with a flair for display across the school, as our 'display champions' who role-model, inspire, support and train others . . . we constantly sell the benefits of display for learning and,

even when we are very busy we don't let standards slip . . .
like all key levers for school improvement, you can't afford
to be complacent!

These are the key messages for us all; commit to making the learning
environment as good as it possibly can be and the impact on the learning
community will be significant. Display *for learning* enables students to
feel that they are valued and appreciated, and that their achievements are
recognized and celebrated. It supports and enables learning in classrooms
and transforms how a school communicates its core values and beliefs. Put
simply: getting display right enhances pedagogy and getting the environment
right values and nurtures every child's ability to achieve and succeed. We
have the tools to do it and there is no better incentive!

Appendix 1

Celebrating achievement display policy

The Compton has placed significant emphasis on celebrating the achievements of students. Students' achievements have been recognized and celebrated in order to improve motivation and develop an achievement culture within the school. A significant part of this shift has included the introduction of corridor boards to celebrate achievements.

The board should contain:

1. Photographs of a minimum of six students across KS3 and KS4. Each department should aim to balance gender, ability, etc. Students should be chosen according to effort, work, progress or extracurricular involvement.
2. Written commentary explaining why these students have been selected as achievers.
3. Model examples of their work.
4. Key words summarizing their achievements.
5. The school motto and school logo.

The board should be changed:

Once a term to provide an opportunity for other students to be celebrated.

The department identifies achieving students by allowing staff to discuss the issue once a term at department meetings, which are also an opportunity to share good practice and positive student experiences.

The department will be responsible for changing corridor displays in rotation throughout the year.

Note: This will not replace the Headteacher's awards or Department awards. Instead it allows for a range of students to be recognized as achieving.

Important

Because of child protection issues students' names must not be placed directly next to photographs of them. Instead names should be written collectively in a box at the bottom of the display.

Appendix 2

History / RE display agreement

Below is a simple checklist of the main things our rooms should have on display:

- Student-friendly NC Level Descriptors (these have already been produced and will simply need to be photocopied and mounted if not already in place).
- Marking symbols (as above, already created).
- Student-friendly book monitoring code.
- Display of History key words . . . It might be an idea to try to go for a predominant, but not exclusive, year-related focus for each room.
- To continue our promotion of Literacy across the curriculum, one display in each room should have this as its focus, e.g. a word wall of relevant words, an extended writing frame, a bank of connectives, etc.
- It is also worth considering having a display with an IT focus and possibly using this as an opportunity to include some numeracy.
- One display board per room should be dedicated to RE.
- We will spend our meeting time producing a really eye-catching WWII theme that lets everyone know they're entering History – this is definitely something on which we could put our heads together!

When planning and preparing displays please remember:

- Their purpose. It is lovely to display students' work but only as a teaching tool, i.e. an enlarged, annotated piece of work – sheets of essays may look good, but rarely will students be able to learn incidentally from them.
- Follow the guidelines for creating effective displays.
- If you are stuck for ideas, copy diagrams from text books – our KS3 texts have some ideal examples.
- Finally, after all your hard work, cover your display with plastic – this will prolong its life and make yours easier too.

Appendix 3

Display policy / environment for learning

1. Aims

- The physical environment should positively affect and augment the school curriculum, providing a stimulating and exciting learning environment. It should underpin an ethos of high expectations by drawing attention to and celebrating:
  - good examples of students' work
  - pride in successful activities
  - informing, motivating and teaching learning
- Attractive display conveys a message about the school's purpose and culture and the school's indoor physical environment should be utilized to consolidate and extend learning.
- Display is key in creating a positive climate; an exciting environment makes for an excited child.

2. Responsibilities

- A member of SLT has overall responsibility for display.
- Heads of Department are responsible for coordinating display in their departmental rooms and display outside their rooms in the corridors.
- Classroom teachers will, however, have overall responsibility for the care of display in their own teaching rooms.
- Pastoral displays are delegated to HOYs and appropriate staff. Once a week the relevant tutor will also be responsible for ensuring their form provide materials for a weekly new board.
- The reprographics officer will assist in preparing and maintaining display boards.

3. Displays in classrooms

Should engage student attention and interest them. Each classroom should aim to have the following types of display:

- displays to aid learning which teachers can refer to in the lesson, e.g. glossaries, maps, diagrams, etc.
- outline course structure, e.g. syllabus summaries, NC levels, grade boundaries
- help students assess their own learning and model ways they can improve
- stimulate further enquiry
- consolidate learning in other ways, e.g. model answers and examples
- create a sense of awe and wonder
- utilize the classroom environment to its full potential using the ceiling, windows and doors and utilizing 3D artefacts
- celebrate good examples of student work
- promote inclusivity by reflecting the achievements of different groups of students and ability ranges

The following are displays that are essential to effective student learning:

- assessment for learning objectives and outcomes cards
- accelerated learning symbols to allow students to demonstrate their level of understanding
- level descriptor board
- celebration of students' achievement
- seating plans
- washing line

Boards should be changed twice a year and washing lines should be changed half-termly. Please see staff guide to display for further information.

4. Displays in the corridor

Corridor display should include:

- a celebrating achievement board (see separate policy for further information)
- boards that reinforce topics taught in the curriculum area
- a work-related learning board specific to the department area

Their purpose is to:

- reinforce the school ethos
- supplement classroom display
- orientate visitors, clearly defining a subject area in the school, e.g. Welcome to the English Department
- provide information – syllabus requirements, coursework deadlines, sporting events, etc.
- reflect current affairs

5. Guidelines on creating a good display

Plan and prepare well by:

- completely stripping the board of the previous display
- using complementary colours on display boards
- backing resources twice
- keeping it simple – do not overcrowd boards
- using a border around the display board
- using a large bold font type readable from a distance
- ensuring titles and key words are written in at least font size 72
- focusing on one topic
- balancing layout – level, symmetrical
- using large, bold images
- using photographs, particularly of students
- having an explanation to put the display in context

Notes: Display materials can be obtained from the resources officer.

6. The school environment

Maintenance of the corridors

- Displays should be kept in good condition and will need to be checked and repaired – use of plastic covering can help to preserve the life of a display.
- Corridors should be kept tidy and free of rubbish.
- Any marks or graffiti in corridors should be reported to the caretaker to remove as soon as possible.

Maintenance of the classroom

- Visual clutter inhibits learning. Cluttered environments can impair cognition, therefore it is vital that classrooms are physically neat before a learning session.
- Ensure that equipment not being used is stored in boxes away from the front of the classroom.
- Do not cover the wall with copious pieces of paper. Use boards to categorize topics.
- At least once a half-term take an honest stock of your classroom, discard materials no longer used, change key words, remove student work.
- Classroom furniture should be checked for marks and chewing gum and if found these should be removed as soon as possible.
- Recycling bins are provided for waste paper.

7. Monitoring

- Observation forms allow recording of comments on classroom display and environment.
- The period from the start of the year until Open Evening is when the condition and quality of all corridor and classroom displays need to be checked.
- HODs to include display on department agendas once a term.

References

1. The Children's Plan

www.dcsf.gov.uk/publications/childrensplan/downloads/The_Childrens_Plan.pdf

'children and young people learn in inspiring and high quality environments': paragraph 4.116, p. 108.

'children need the right environment to be able to learn and thrive': paragraph 4.85, p. 101.

2. The Compton School, Barnet

The Compton School, Barnet, is a non selective 11–16 comprehensive in an area of North London with a significant number of selective, single-sex and voluntary-aided faith schools. Entry is based on proximity to the school and the school is hugely oversubscribed, with over 820 applications for 180 places in 2008/9. The multicultural intake draws from a mixed socio-economic catchment and 19 per cent of the students are on free school meals. The school is situated in the middle of a large council estate. However, many families in private housing will move to live very near to the school in order to secure a place for their child. Twenty-nine per cent of students are on the SEN register including over 4 per cent with a statement of educational needs. This means the school has an SEN intake which is significantly above the borough average.

The school is a Technology College and also has Training School and Leading Edge status, and is second and third specialism as a high-performing specialist school. In 2003, and again in 2007, the HMCI Report placed The Compton School on its list of outstanding schools. Indeed in 2005 it was included on a shorter list as being one of the most successful schools in the country. In the 2006 Ofsted inspection the school achieved 'outstanding' status in all 24 areas inspected. It is now one of only a handful of schools nationally with three successive outstanding Ofsted inspections.

In 2008 the GCSE results, at 73 per cent 5+ A*–C, with an intake estimated by FFT to gain 66 per cent, placed the school in the top 7 per cent nationally for progress.

It is always difficult to single out individual reasons for a school's success. Ofsted notes that primarily the effectiveness of the school is due to the 'Inspirational Leadership of the Headteacher, supported by a committed and extremely talented team that underpins the school's exceptional success'. In addition to this fundamental feature it is also interesting to note that the environment was identified as a key feature of success, the report describing display as 'superb' and stating that it is evident 'in all classrooms'. The fact that all members of the Compton community believe in the value of display is what makes it so powerful. There are no 'lone' voices. Every board in every classroom mirrors the genuine care and pride felt for and by students during their career at The Compton. It is this that enables students to make the exceptional progress that they do.

3. Mike Fleetham

Mike Fleetham is an educational consultant and established author, working with teachers and learners worldwide to help make education more effective and enjoyable. He specializes in the practical, down-to-earth applications of thinking skills, multiple intelligences, learning styles and change management in educational and business settings. His Thinking Classroom concept and associated books, website and training have inspired and re-inspired thousands of teachers.

Mike's website offers up-to-date information and free resources: www.thinkingclassroom.co.uk

4. The Fischer Family Trust

The Fischer Family Trust (FFT) is an independent, not-for-profit charitable trust. While its main focus is education, the Trust also undertakes and supports a range of other health, maritime and conservation projects in the UK. Since 2001, FFT, through its Data Analysis Project, has provided local authorities in England and Wales with a range of value-added analyses to support self-evaluation and estimates to inform target setting. Over the last seven years, the use of FFT data has become embedded in the classroom and is used successfully by teachers and senior leaders in many schools to support school improvement. FFT data is also used by the National Strategies, the DCSF (Department for Children, Schools and Families) Academies Division and the Specialist Schools and Academies Trust. More recently, FFT has developed a range of online reports – available from https://www.fftlive.org – allowing schools and Local Authorities to access FFT data directly from the Web.

If you would like to know more about how FFT data can help your school then please visit www.fischertrust.org. For access to FFT data, usernames and passwords for FFT Live or for any other queries/support then please contact your Local Authority directly. A list of Local Authority contacts is available from the FFT website.

Index

D

E

F, G, H

I, K

L